WANNA HEAR... LISTEN!

ADDING THOSE SPRINKLES TO YOUR LIFE...

GURANSH SINGH

notionpress.com

INDIA • SINGAPORE • MALAYSIA

1

I ain't where I hanker to be;

It's all because of thee.

Was just like a sweet ephemeral flow,

Which was destined to fleet away.

~g

2

Nature is a creation of God,

Hence, the most beautiful one.

We hardly notice the good-looking clouds,

And not appreciate the pleasing Sun.

Moon being the brightest one,

Is hardly noticed though.

All around a busy world,

We are confined in it you know.

People are busy in their tiring world,

Have no time to notice the flowers curled.

They have become genuine robots,

Besides, they are themselves the creation of the Almighty Lord…

~g 

Don't be a member of the latent,
It was destined for what it was.
Make the veiled a purposeful one,
For it's the only duty you are bestowed with…

~g

My choices were never defined,
They kept moulding until they finally perished…

~g

I cherished recalling the trail;
Emerging strong from the frail;
Trying to elude the stains;
Rather remembering the mounted gains…

~g

The walls were painted now and then;
To highlight their presence in the world beyond your
    ken;
The scars concealed in the latent coat;
Who could bear the flung out if it evoked…

~g

This mortal portrayed a tender bird;
Which awaits a wind to buoy his flight.

~g

I condemn to plead in a world known the greed.

~g

9

Diversified by creed;

United by purpose;

Segregated by many;

To divide the commune;

Amassing their clout;

To make us attune.

Veiling their motive;

To wrangle among;

Oppressed by the riches;

To exploit the mum;

Who got his rights to clung?

It was rather a vague thought which was fleeting flung…

~g

If I were you;

was I just a diminished hue or an entity whose presence
was hard to subdue…

~g

I loved walking with the wind while settling in the rain; Enveloped with the extremes did never go in vain; A lot gained when the oppression took over the reign; It thus made me flush the regrets in the drain...

~g

Autumn for the nature was indeed a decree; Shedding
of leaves as if a burden set free...

~g

Trying to answer your derailed 'what if's', you would succumb your in hand 'what could's'…

~g

Two lives set well apart;
While one tends to fleet between the two.

~g

Many asked what led me hear;
I said some uncertain affair which was hard to bear.

~g

What seemed an idyllic was never a though; It enshrouded the truth to lure you slow. This ocean evolved to become a place of disguise; where one who can bear while the other who cries...

~g

17

A pleasant night is all I crave,

When the world trodden, leaves me apart.
While all my hope is devoured onto;
I still sought help weeping in despair.

The questions put in the dark urged a depart;
It too answered with a fainting mellow.
Atleast a fleeting dream did me a favour;
Helped me meet you and rather express too !

The night's offer was indeed a need;
Which dwelled me into and separate the weed.
All I then recall is a bout of content;
Which accompanied the soul to never rest in resent.

I wished if the day was mine as the night belonged to me
And I believe, it soon will be.
Until then, a pleasant night is all I crave;
When the world trodden, leaves me apart…

~g

Death was indeed a stranger to him but it embraced
him as if it knew the soul better than he himself had…

~g

19

My rightful childhood was hence a fleeting dream;
Which I abandoned so soon that it went astray.
Did I lose my fun-loving years that early?
I often raise this question yet with a mandate sigh.

I am still a teen but can't figure what led me mean;
Maybe to know the world I was a bit too keen.
Perhaps this bout of maturity had never dwindled;
The smoothening of its tangles was enough to rekindle.

What else could I have done besides a deep nosedive;
The sharks there as well won't leave me alive.
Was my childhood really a see-through pane;
Or happen a disguised which I didn't even realise and
drained in the vain?

~g

20

The Perish

A lot more accompanied this yellow mortal;
When it buried in the mud and realised what it had.
An empty hand and no kindred;
He wished to act better with a wholesome dread.

It's then encountered the real truths;
When the turn he got was eventually over.
God forbid its malice then;
The soul now fled to disturb the men.

It craved for a longing peace;
When was then provided in an eternal rest.
Happen he wished for the well;
It could all have been a better story.

The epitaph read with all its disguise;
For the stone laid there couldn't evince.
The mortal's too couldn't speak now much;
It already had misled as such.

It still dwelled it's past to recall what it had cast;
For in its present times these echoes didn't last.
It never realised in the time of a cherish;
The man still was afraid of the perish…

~g

21

Football

I rolled on the lush green bed;
And swivelled in the air like thread.
Being profoundly dumb, could do nothing;
Bearing those thrusts with those powerful pushes apart.

Those heavy legs were enough to jitter;
A sphere bloated with air.
I levitated with free kicks and shuddered with heads;
Could I do anything or just to rest in a shed?

Your elated faces were enough for me;
I hit the nets and it uplifted your glee.
I am the football with brought a chill spree;
I still wonder if anyone cares about me?

~g

22

A Final Goodbye

Felt like a withered touch to say goodbye;
When all seems well and there's a sudden cry.
Even the cloud wept and coveted your hearty laugh;
Well, it's all so clear on my behalf.
I hope not too soon we again say that word;
As if fishes never wanted the water stirred.
When all seems parched and there's a pleasant shower;
Every soul hankers to sit under the leafy bower.
Such felt the cool under that breezy shade;
As if the almighty himself was ready with his aid.
After such an abrupt fade;
I still never wanted a farewell bade.
Perhaps being loved and lost was a better claim;
Than never loved and still blame…

~g

23

The Memory Lane

Happen you would mention me in your history;
Say with tangling thoughts and untold lies.
And rather may abandon me in that very gloom;
I still won't mind that cause' for me;
You still possessed some room.
Wonder my ruly pop ups still upset you;
But you rather did never want to subdue them.
Perhaps you wanted to see me broken;
With all such despair and lowered eyes.
Hence so weakened by my desperate cries.
That would still not happen my friend;
Like air itself, I still shall rise…

~g

24

The Love For Black

I wonder why black likes me;

Or say I like black.

For a faint stain has a presence all about;

If I had this sheath what could happen, I doubt.

Some curling wrinkles which were hardly ironed;

Ever could make their way through.

As if like me it had borne a lot but still couldn't squeak.

Maybe I loved black cause' it hid all my malice in its doom;

It suited me well and helped in my gloom !

What's a better partner one would crave for;

It's all black on this side still.

Those reds and blues please learn from the black;

It ditched others with its wit;

Still my face was suffused with a lit.

How could I ever abandon this lovely black?

It was indeed a single shade yet so colourful…

~g

What seemed a gem was hard to condemn;
You possessed a brave heart to fade from them.
One what often seems a fleeting passenger;
Sticks to your shadow and ever walks slow.

I too came across a hollow vessel;
Which was indeed so vacant to fill my exhaust.
It made me realise what had made me here;
And soon would help me in a world so severe.

Some people just become a part of you;
Happen you are alone left, bear and pass through.
Care for them, my beloved and never feel them spare;
Until they eventually fade and you are succumbed to despair…

~g

26

Beauty's Beauty

Beauty cannot simply be expressed;
I tried it over but was left so vexed.
Beauty lies everywhere;
But is sought by the one who really cares.

The words would never portray its hue;
For to pour its rain, you couldn't easily subdue.
Beauty itself craves an eye;
And wished if it would never bade her a bye.

I noticed beauty in a latent cause;
And I too imagined whom it was.
Beauty's beauty cannot simply be expressed;
I tried it over but was left so vexed…

~g

27

The one bewitched by another;
Seldom offered a pleasant cause.
What it Interred was then a chaos;
Which the latent dealt without an across.

It often wondered the sight so bliss;
Which it craved forever and craves still.
It felt that alone so left with a heavy tread;
Only hope could suffice that loner too dead.

Left with nothing, it masked to pretend;
Though it never was endowed to act that well.
I pity that one for it could be me;
All ends blocked, it soon should flee.

Ever weeping, it though held a smile;
It always wished for its perish without an aghast.
What was left to fleet was nothing so precise;
It too paid its cherish for a dwindling price.

Its rejoicing moments were ever tightly clung;
Though in vain, could they still be flung?
At its time to end, it happened to make a wish so last;
For having you besides would have a mellow cast !

~g

28

Being underwater seems like dwelling in a soul,
The deeper you dive;
There's still to explore in another whole.
The scorching beams paved their way;
Still the through it went couldn't reach the basal.
The consuming darkness with that force like urge;
Tangled you in its gloomy sphere.
Some mysteries underwater still couldn't be solved;
There were left there for another sojourn.
Diving deep, the latent silenced;
Though it couldn't calm the internal beats.
Soon enough, they too would be unheard;
Eventually putting me to an eternal rest…

~g

29

If I were a chaos, then you were my contain;

Though being a wanderlust;

I never realized my destination was you.

If you were an ocean;

Then I cherished the waves but terrified to swim.

What set us apart was indeed a receding shore;

which was enough to maintain an enticing distance

~g

30

I once went to far flung shore;
With deepening horizons immersing with the wave's
roar.
All it allayed to my long-trodden dismay;
Synced with the waters which soon seemed to ebb
away.

Those in your sight were often there to fleet;
Besides being a menace, they too knew to cheat.
As the wind renounced its firming authority;
Quivered this being with a bit hope in paucity.

Happen I wasn't the only one lane in the dumps:
Though the only with who stayed rested, flumped;
As the water flowed through my awkward schlep;
So did I conclude no one was to help…

~g

31

The One So Faithful

Many came across in these lively scenes;

Maybe to assess the world, I was a bit too keen.

Some clung tight to your moving shadows;

While some had to leave as they were winnowed.

You played with a few,

While some played with you;

It seems just an array to help you imbue.

Most manoeuvred and held your side;

Still, you knew the one who could guide.

Happen the ones which ditched you ago;

Were also a part to prepare for woes.

To the one who understood you glaring explain;

Dealt and accepted the pains lain in the memory lane.

Amidst a bustling crowd;

It's hues reached you with a no longer shroud.

Somehow knew when no longer talked;

You still held an attract which was indeed no mock.

It's presence plenished the vacant and made you complete;

Such lovely feelings aren't often to fleet.

The only among the known who saw you cry;
Whose absence you regarded as a dejecting awry.
I miss those faces known to none;
No one said nor did I who was that faithful one...

~g

32

Everything past and ahead seemed planned for you;

Still beware for whatever you do.

Often what held a rightest intention;

Was enveloped inside an internal drive.

What you did in this part of the sphere;

Imbedded In an eternal dimension ever so far.

Your deeds, you actions- these ain't really any jargons;

Their piercing offerings won't leave any room for the pardons.

They could either heal or destroy;

For it is often said that karma is indeed a bad boy...

~g

33

The night feels darker today;

Trying to engulf me in its gloom.

I need someone along but I don't know whom;

Happen someone like me is searching too, this is what I assume.

Alone I have to bear, I would better surrender to my doom;

Though wandering like this did help my soul exhume.

The day too had an uncanny loneliness;

With everyone along, I couldn't control my quirks.

Borne a lot though still unfamiliar with how that works;

When everything around evolves, I feel like a decaying corpse.

An unknown plight which often perturbs;

I want to yet have no reason to perk.

You got your ways and you got your quirks

But the one got my heart and that's why it works…

~g

34

Give time to yourself buddy;
Listen to yourself, you ain't unlucky.
When you change your envelope muddy;
You realise it had some stains to study.

I perused that period, what happened then;
I was left unheard among a lot of men.
No force deterred my degrade rather time;
Which healed me through and washed the grime.

Just keep moving and hold a firm step;
When nothing except yourself could stop the schlep.
Everything would unravel while your emotions were
on the ebb;
You could no longer be entangled in that dreadful
web...

~g

Would I ever be the one or just among the ones;
This question is what I had to shun.
What if things unravelled in a flurry;
Would it ever help or just worsen the scurry.
What if some junctures were never planned to be;
For a personal self, I never could uplift my glee.
A familiar face which carved its outline;
Asked me these questions which felt so sublime.
Though I couldn't answer the qualms raised;
Happen the enchanting presence left me fazed.
How shall I deliver my laden words;
To the one I should tell could then feel stirred.

~g

36

What happens too often is a flux to bear;
Supposedly it had a motive to help you gear.
For me it's helping overcoming some fears;
Which rather so often I never dared.

Held my sight to see if there's anyone there;
Left abandoned even don't know where.
Well, that was fine for there's no one to care;
No one to share that I was better aware.

A piercing voice then suggested to stay here;
I said don't worry if I vanish somewhere.
He said there's some wild animals just beware;
I said with an aghast Well that is fine for there's no one
to care.

Then we talked upon what he had to bear;
I listened the keen voice which craved an ear.
Now it was my turn and I had to share;
As soon as I did, he was succumbed to despair…

~g

37

I Always Chose The Paper

May these winds blow me away as well;
No one I found who could help me unravel;
Nothing's a better claim then rather to quell;
Withered as if there's nothing In which I could dwell.

Happened for a reason, I knew before;
Some wounds leave a pain which no one can cure;
I know I am not the only one who bore;
But I encountered somethings, I wish I don't explore anymore.

If I were ever to split into two;
The latent could divide and helped to make it through;
Whatever has happened shall have motive to explain too;
When you are despaired, the words would feel better which ever were due.

So, I loved waking with the wind while settling in the rain;
Enveloped with the extremes did never go in vain;

A lot gained when the oppression took over the reign;
It thus made me flush the regrets in the drain.

I wonder why all those met weren't often that close;
Pretending to them is what I chose;
What I then held was a distance to maintain;
Though walking in those streets, I still feel chained.
I have a thousand things to express,
though I still chose a refrain
Perhaps loved and lost was a better claim
Then never loved and still blame…

~g

38

I catch you with a diminishing hue;
Sometimes, I even forget what else I have to do.
Maybe you are the only one with whom I tend to glue;
In you I shall live, in you I shall flew.

You seem among the few I wanna delve into;
Happen you know more than them what I had gone through.
When I met you, I recall the despair I threw;
For you seemed the only path I ought to pursue.

Though talking to you has some long-led queues;
Still, I often wish to mount up the clues.
I never thrived only strived, that's how I grew;
That is why the odyssey needs to be started anew.

I noticed the cues still doubted if they were true;
Don't know why, though I often feel screwed.
I regret the acts I couldn't undo;
Eventually my heart is often laden with rue…

~g

45

The face had the filth while you kept blaming the mirror...

~g

40

The one I remember who held a sweet smile;
Happen was indeed the only one.
An etched memory often flings out;
When I can no longer subdue it's presence.
I recall it's echoes which resonate in my ear;
Perhaps it had become a part, I was no longer aware.
There's still a lot stuff to unravel;
While I suppose, between us, it would still dispose.
It held something I could no longer oppose;
Rather it expressed something, I never supposed.
A lot more was seen when it's been so clear;
So shall I still expect from you what I never dared?
The unfinished talks which we partly shared;
Raised some questions I felt in your glare.
I might not be the one you craved to delve into;
Just as you withered away, maybe I found your clue.
Just passing those smiles wasn't enough for me;
When I wanted to evade and set myself free.
You made an effort to clung me tight;
Though picturing you then was enough to buoy my flight...

~g

41

It Just Gets Truer...

I have had a terrible past;
With such echoes, maybe it was bound to last.
What happened all around, I never dared to ask;
Happen I thought with this, I too shall pass.

Despaired fleets met along the way;
Until they fleeted away and went astray.
A lot was borne under an oppressive sway;
When no ear was ready to hear my say.

Things gradually changed when they needed me;
To set them free from their muddling spree.
Happen with those false claims, I learnt to pretend;
This useful quirk would indeed never come to an end.

Moulded so much, I forget if I was still true;
Maybe not, my heart is still laden with rue.
Since then, I never crossed to memory lane;
It was all me, there's no one to blame...

~g

42

Finishing Touches

I drew something and wondered along;

If those shades could ever add life to a frame.

Being patient all through, an answer unmasked ;

"Yes" it was, awhile I sketched a beaut.

An entity emerged from an eternal rest;

With those piercing eyes glaring, I was taken aback.

A hazy face when i groped around, couldn't reflect as such;

It then struck to all my notice that something was amiss.

Then what occurred to me was bout of questions;

For how could I carve what lay in its beyond.

A quirky brush with those mingling colours;

Did a favour and solved the qualm.

As it's expressions unravelled so did my tangles;

When none of us wished to be put asunder.

The black and white was now a hue;

It was made as such, my heart abandoned the rues.

I completed it with content though it demanded something;
Conveyed with a wink~some finishing touches indeed…

~g

43

I forgot those days when those tears ever flowed;
Happen you came in my life to help me recall…

~g

44

I was never laden with such a rue;
That whatever you said didn't seem that true.
I wish I could convey through those impassive words;
I still didn't believe myself being that absurd.

I met for a reason and would detach for one too;
Whatever we had then never will glue.
I hope those lines could ever be taken back;
They took a toll on me and fed onto whatever I lacked.

I was made aware that wasn't trance;
You questioned me often with a perturbing glance.
No answer I had for my unruly state;
Maybe what formed the latter now attracted hate.

Felt like a decaying corpse while some fed on me;
Never talked in the eye to reflect a muddling spree.
I met for a reason and would detach for one too;
Never dared to ask if fleet to soon.

Leave these words, I often trusted the pen;
To convey something even beyond your Ken.…

~g

45

Years lapsed in a broad time frame;
You too know what happened being naive and lame.
Not just the remarks to which I kept a mum;
Also the emotions I possessed which weren't flung.
I learnt to keep a shallow mind;
Too often into which I don't drown.
It wasn't a tryst to be ever borne;
Eventually what had seemed a forlorn was an object of scorn.
A fainting mellow echoed again;
Everything changed since it's reign.
A story concocted wasn't now in thrall;
Left being astray, I never allowed the gall.
A lying mirror only showed the skin;
Abandon its presence and realise what's within.
What dried the tears was the scorching heat;
The least ember left would reignite to give them a treat.
Good enough for an awkward trawl;
Now just hope that it's bad won't meet its evil to engage in a brawl...

~g

Some feelings I wished could never be subdued;
Some hues I shaded which eventually imbued.
What else shall I offer to that far flung urge;
Maybe it was nearing me gradually while I distanced apart…

~g

I don't know what I mean to you
To me, it's more than what my pen has to do
You told me what you ever went through
I am glad you trusted cause' there's only a few

~g

48

Things change, they really do;
What first rests so secure with you, will just pass through.
It ain't something to regret for;
Just a stain you don't want anymore.

Those fond memories would demand an escape;
When the one who felt so close would fleet...
For the one who searched for you all through;
Now feared facing you in a crowd.

I have never known where I came from;
Just lay down in the dumps and met someone, and this is what I have become.
I wished i was a love poetry;
At least then someone could express me in itself...

Thing feel truer, they really do;
Until you read this again, for now it just passed through you.

~g

Imagine me being you;
Knowing exactly what's residing in you;
Though my heart being laden with rue;
I would flee before you ever knew...

~g

50

I never thought we could be such good friends;

For what I had lacked could barely be mend.

Days paced in a queer blend;

Soon your absence felt as if a thrusting scend.

What else should I have done than rather to pretend;

To convey what had made me love at the very end.

I trusted someone besides what lay penned;

The hues which imbued weren't possible to be kenned.

I am not quite sure if all of this, you could easily apprehend;

But believe me, there's always the best for you I intend.

I lay silent whenever your exhaust needed a vent;

Happen I knew somehow you had borne to contend.

I never want you to be ever so distant;

So that a goodbye from you is all I expect at the end…

~g

51

I lost myself just to find you;

Though with those weaklings tied, I felt even worse.

Everything was a chill between us;

Seemed just to pretend as if.

Since long I have been there;

Just in the hope that I was even a part.

A part which couldn't be put asunder;

Maybe I was just a hue which was destined for a diminishing cast.

When everything's placed, I still feel something's amiss;

I barely could convey it so chose to bear the muddle.

I was sure, I couldn't find anyone better;

Still, I preferred that enticing distance.

I lay silent to hear you speak, with an ever sweet mellow;

Soon no one would be there, while I would hear the echo.

Maybe I was never a part;

So just to find myself again, I ought to lose you...

~g

52

Who knew

Who knew I could be you;
Just as same, coloured with that hue.
Who knew I could be your part;
So truly enough, none wished a depart.
Who knew we could be close;
Together we shall defy the foes.
Who knew it wasn't that easy;
For me, talking to you was always a bit queasy.
Who knew i wasn't alone;
I am glad I wasn't left unknown.
Who knew we were never so far;
As we just pretended to avoid a scar.
Who knew i could soon feel distant;
To you, I would have never existed from that instant.
Who knew if that day could ever come;
Just ensure then what it helped us become.
Who knew if those days passed would ever have a cast;
I never knew what I meant, maybe just "another person" who didn't last.
Who knew what plans the destined had for us;
Though we both knew the answers already...

~g

53

A lie carved its own contain;

Its emerging hue makes a truth mundane.

When all those trails dumped the efforts in vain;

I am afraid if I still could be a mention in your memory lane.

While what flung out did not intend to relay;

What seems a better claim is just an inevitable delay.

A sublime outline which urged to answer;

The questions which lay beyond its reach.

Less did it know, it was just a hazy envelope;

Of lies and enigmas, it had itself developed.

With every truth I could lose you, while just a lie helped me held;

The end had it all~

I told you nothing...still you believed everything.

~g

Loved trawling through the streets of gloom;
For I supposedly knew the light would then feel
sharper…

~g

55

I wonder from where these sweet sounds emerge;
of mellow tone they carried to diverge.
my heart leaps up at that sight to behold;
of gaudy hues which brighten the sky.
()
So as the rainbow coloured so it spirited the life;
elating glimpses which made you alive.
Cloudless climes yet twinkling skies;
was all to belove in your hazy eyes.
()
serene places for the chirping creatures;
was like an eternal rest after a strenuous reach.
dripping water which pounds the rocks;
felt as if a curing elixir which healed the perturbing knocks...

~g

Produced by the situation;
Moulded by the offerings;
Manufactured by tyranny;
Refined by the experience;
Bargained by the jolts;
And indeed, sold to the fleeting hopes…

~g

Sorry, I never told you what I had in me, confined;
You asked for it several times but what lay in that pit
is now beyond my find.
I could either grin and bear or vent out the truth;
But I still won't feel free abandoning you in the ruth.

~g

What had seemed so beloved is hard to forget;
You still crave but are bound to regret;
Never confessed what's resting in those lies;
Yet we both knew all through those truthful eyes...

~g 

59

Hankerings being lame was never a rue;
The ones not fulfilled joined the queue;
A half deterred to muddle the hue;
The latter envisioned what it could ensue…

~g

60

I glared at a pane to all my shock;
perhaps that wasn't the better claim.
Maybe I sought a better reflect;
But it was supposedly due to a hidden deflect.

The window was indeed on the verge of a shatter;
Happen It could no longer bear.
I never evinced a tint still it had often felt;
Who was the one I could no longer imagine !?

~g

My Future Self To Me

Hey memory lane, how you feeling?
Oh wait ! I better knew with what you were dealing.
Your desires, your feelings you kept at bay,
In order to unravel your eventful stay.

Stop being a fake and don't ever pretend,
Or your evincing powers will gradually end.
The thundering jolts which made you astray,
Unleash your potential and push them away.

Cleanse your clutters so the filth never comes near,
Get ready brother ! Some chaos too is lined up here.
Accept your powers which are one of a kind,
Calm your breathe along with your mind.

The deeds you had done got nothing but hate,
No one knew except your fate.
Why not this stagnant heart ever flow?
What endured it through was indeed a blow.

The link with that one was nothing but divine,
May he bless you into his shrine.
I still find myself wandering in the woods,
For if my youth only knew if my age only could…

~g

62

Often what I neared to cherish;

With a gradual wither, I knew it would perish.

Knowing exactly what could happen;

I still didn't know what for me will make the vacant plenish.

Maybe a day awaits when I no one noticed the blemish;

How long shall I pretend;

With those weaklings tied and truths confide...I forgot what's an embellish...

How bad if felt when you neared someone while it was destined to distance. I knew it well to often confine myself…

Eventually I shall greet you as all loveable things are meant to be. But rather;

With a poem on my mind and an often sob which awaits that moment...,

~g

I don't just want to be another sweet little cameo in your eventful life, maybe a bigger one which holds a presence even after this play has come to an end..."

~g

64

People come, they pass by;
The ones gone, for them don't cry.
Those who sticked by your side, never bade them a bye.
Whose absence you would always regard as a dejecting awry.
Somethings lay abandoned with you, which simply could never be denied;
They mounted up soon, and exhausted you inside;
They heard you through until had a relief sigh;
While you hoped the end to this bond is never nigh.
Ever so often it has been on the sly.
While you ought to treasure their memories for aye
Their departure so new would be enveloped in lies
While then you won't resist those drops in the eye...

~g

When my hunger to live would not be fed;
Whatever you felt would rest with you.
I lay silent in that shallow pit;
Unravelling mysteries even without a breathe...

~g

Everyone's ready to listen until a keen voice pierces them through...

~g

67

Hollowness;
As if this definite depth is fathomless...

Drowning;
In this oceanic sphere full of fears...

Hope;
Which I am losing every moment passing by...

Help;
What I tend to seek behind this masked face...

Lost;
In an eerie gloom where serenity is a prohibition...

~g

Don't imperil your present for your future or your past,

Your past was a teacher which had to be embraced

While the future is veiled, filled with the "unknowns" yet to be encountered…

~g

I cerebrate why these stars blink,
For they seem to ask me something.
I hanker if I could decipher them,
And learn about their intriguing curiosities…

~g

70

They both met on my way towards life;

Happen to just cure what I had done to myself.

While one was just met in disguise;

Who wished me with her, I too shall rise.

The other so calming just felt a receding shore;

I tried nearing her soon, though the enticing distance had become a mandate.

Time passed with its gradual wink;

Now dwindled alone thru my awkward schlep.

Perhaps as all stars were to disappear one day;

With their diminishing lights, I grew alone in darkness.

Although as I just looked up at that empty sky;

I felt nothing except an urge the embrace the sublime.

Finally, though I chose someone who made me complete;

So, I chose myself !

Now I just wish, I don't get truer about people;

Rather I won't, they seldom ask to unravel…

~g

71

I just kept walking and was joined by many
now I just keep growing...shedding the ones who have been hindering my leap
more often, people don't stay by your side, they just promise you that fleeting comfort to eventually fleet away

~g